I Couldn't Wait to Tell You

I Couldn't Wait to Tell You

Ethyl Katz

Writers Club Press
San Jose New York Lincoln Shanghai

I Couldn't Wait to Tell You

All Rights Reserved © 2000 by Ethyl Katz

No part of this book may be reproduced or transmitted in any form or by any means, graphic, electronic, or mechanical, including photocopying, recording, taping, or by any information storage retrieval system, without the permission in writing from the publisher.

Writers Club Press
an imprint of iUniverse.com, Inc.

For information address:
iUniverse.com, Inc.
620 North 48th Street, Suite 201
Lincoln, NE 68504-3467
www.iuniverse.com

Cover design by Terri Katz Kasimov

Excerpts from *The Secret Garden*, by Frances Hodgson Burnett

ISBN: 0-595-12769-X

Printed in the United States of America

To my grandchildren Garrett, Meryl, and Dashiell who bring me sunshine every day. It humbles me to realize that it will be through their eyes and from their lips that my progeny will hear this story.

Acknowledgements

There are two people associated with book publishing to whom I am deeply indebted. They are Michael Harkavy and Denise Sterrs. Each, upon reading my manuscript, took the time and interest to encourage and motivate me to continue on this project. Their now dog-eared letters sustained me.

Thanks to my children-by-birth and children-by-marriage Michael and Wanda, Alan and Jerry, Kyle and Warren and to my niece, Terri, for their encouragement and because they too, refused to let me give up.

My heartfelt appreciation to Lilli, Tobie, Judy, Caroline, Marty, Paula, Virginia and Inga, my writing workshop buddies, for their constructive suggestions and to Bernard Selling, our leader, whose critiques were always "right on."

I also wish to laud research scientists whose tireless work brings those challenged by cancer new treatments and new hope. And I mourn for those who were challenged too soon.

To Sam, my ever-loving husband, thanks for remaining my most devoted fan, published or not.

And Ilene are you listening? To you, for sharing it all with me.

Introduction

As-sem-blage: A sculptural technique of organizing or composing into a unified whole a group of unrelated and often fragmentary or discarded objects.

The Random House Dictionary of the English Language

Through all the years I spent working at sculpting, enameling, weaving, and ceramics, my sister Ilene would criticize, "This is all well and good, Ethyl, but you're dabbling. It's time for you to focus. You should be working in assemblage or collage. Trust me. I know. That is where your talent lies."

Each time I would protest in defense of my current endeavor, "This is what I want to do, Ilene." I loved sculpting and enameling and weaving and ceramics.

Whenever I visited her in Buffalo, Ilene and I would go to the Albright Knox Art Gallery. Once we saw a Joseph Cornell assemblage exhibit there. We were fascinated and explored with delight each box filled with tiny, odd objects.

As we examined, Ilene scolded, "If you had listened to me years ago when I told you to work in assemblage, who knows, Ethyl? We might be looking at your work now!" A psychologist would probably find it interesting that I didn't at least try. After all, I tried everything else.

But it's never too late. The time has come and now I'm ready to focus. My assemblage series consists of moments in the lives Ilene and I shared from 1930, when Ilene was eight and I a year-and-a-half younger, to 1990 and beyond. Like Cornell's boxes, the bits and pieces of my works are not dark; certainly there is no evil, corruption, treachery, or turmoil here. They are, rather, about what makes those things bearable. Joyous or sad, momentous or mundane, these fleeting fragments are what we remember long after the exhibit has closed.

Assemblage I

"There is a door into the garden—I found it."
The Secret Garden

Prologue

May 27, 1979

My sister died today.
Each day for this last hopeless month I have wished her out of her misery, and each morning I have walked into her hospital room and whispered, "Thank you, God, for one more day."
I don't understand.
All I know is that she died today.
Every day for this last hopeless month I have resented the crisp, smooth, white, hospital sheets covering her wasting body, their tightly tucked corners telling everyone who looks inside, "All is well in this room."
Each morning I walk in and for one brief second I've believed the lie the sheets are telling. Then I remember and loathe those sheets for the truth they try to hide.
All day for each day of this last hopeless month I have sat in the hospital room or in the corridor with Terri and Shelley, my nieces, reading and re-reading, as if they were bibles, Elizabeth Kubler Ross's On Death And Dying and Raymond Moody's Life After Life. Alone, I have wondered if we are grasping at straws to ease our pain. Are we bargaining, "O.K. God, you win, but even if we

can't see her, she'll be alive—somewhere. There is life after life, right? Right?"

God hasn't answered and I am still confused.

Two weeks ago they said, "She won't live out this week. Stay until next Friday for shiva, Ethyl. Then go home. You've been away for two months. You need to go home."

The theys have been very practical.

"There are airline strikes," they said. "Reservations are hard to get. Make one now for that Friday. She'll be gone. You go home to California. Go home."

I did. Make the reservation, that is. But she rallied, and on the Sunday they said she'd die, she spoke to each of us, giving words of advice. Even dying didn't change that old habit.

For those who couldn't understand her mumbling I interpreted. I understood every word and gesture.

For the first time ever, she didn't give me advice.

All she said to me was, "We'll meet in our secret garden."

It was all she had to say. I knew.

That was two weeks ago.

There is more I need to understand. Last Friday, that plane on which I had a reservation crashed on take-off from Chicago sending the two hundred and seventy poor souls aboard to a fiery grave. Was it a coincidence? Was it intervention? If not Ilene's, whose? I don't know.

All I do know is my sister died today.

1930

Ilene and I are almost ready for bed. I'm so hot and sweaty that it's hard to breathe. Mom comes upstairs to tuck us in. She wipes her face on the edge of her dirndl skirt and mutters, "It's like an oven in here. Why don't you just wear your p.j. bottoms and see if that helps?"

Just then Dad comes upstairs and we hear him say to Mom, "It's just too hot and humid. There's no way they can sleep in this heat. Let's all go for a ride and get a Vernors." Ilene and I hold our breaths. We're waiting to hear Mom's answer. We've been to Vernors a few times. We love it.

"You're right," Mom agrees, "maybe it will be cool enough to sleep later."

"Get dressed," she says turning to us. "We're going for a ride."

Ilene is eight years old and I'm six. We hardly ever get to stay up past eight o'clock. We're ready in less than two minutes.

Vernors is on Falls Street, just two blocks from Niagara Falls Park. It looks like a soda fountain, but it isn't. All that squirts out of its shiny silver faucets is something called Vernors Ginger Ale. It tastes good and has lots of bubbles. Some people get a scoop of vanilla ice cream in their Vernors. I would love some in mine but I'm afraid to ask Dad. He might get mad. Then he'll lecture me again about how there is a depression and some people can't even afford the Vernors. The man behind the counter puts the full glasses of ginger ale on trays and all the Dads carry them out to their families waiting in the cars parked out in front on Falls Street.

Everyone parks facing the curb. It's easier to watch all the tourists walking by that way.

Like always, it's nice and cool in front of Vernors tonight. There's always a breeze from the park. You can even hear the roar of the Falls from here.

Dad and Mom are in the front seat of Dad's black Chrysler sedan talking. Mom is holding my sleeping baby brother, Jerry. I'm in back with Ilene and Dina, who is eleven. Ilene and I sit on the edge of the back seat so we can see out the front window. We are racing to see who can count more honeymoon couples walking by.

"There's one," Ilene squeals. "I've got four now."

I look at the couple she points to. "You're cheating. They aren't honeymooners. They don't have on new shoes," I point out.

"They do, too," Ilene retorts. "Mom, aren't those honeymooners over there? They have on new shoes, don't they?" Mom, who is deep in conversation with Dad, glances at the couple and nods.

I don't give up. "Wait, they're walking by now. We'll tell from the bottoms of their shoes." Ilene and I scoot down as far as we can get and still see through the side window. "See, his shoes are dirty on the bottom," I cry. "They aren't honeymooners. They don't count."

"O.K.," Ilene gives in, "but then you can't have that real old couple you counted just because they wore new shoes and had no kids."

We continue to sip and bicker aimlessly. Finally Dina, who considers herself much older than we, almost an adult, can take it no longer. "Dad," she lies, "they're spilling Vernors all over the back seat."

Dad stops talking long enough to say over his shoulder, "Why don't you two get out and stand on the sidewalk in front of the car till you finish?"

Ha, I gloat silently, Dina thinks she's getting us in trouble and by mistake does us a favor. Ilene and I scramble eagerly on to the sidewalk. We hoist ourselves up on the car's front bumper. Ilene climbs up and drapes herself on one of the front fenders. It looks comfortable. I copy her on the other fender.

We both steal fearful glances over our shoulders at Dad. He might not like us climbing all over his car. He and Mom are still talking. He doesn't seem to mind at all.

I can picture Dina spread out on the back seat looking pleased at all the room she now has. Little does she know what she's missing.

Through the straw I gulp my last mouthful of Vernors. The bubbles tickle my nose. This is the life, I think. Here we are sprawled on the fenders as if they were sofas right in the middle of the busiest street in town. It's late at night and instead of being home in bed we're sipping drinks and enjoying the cool breeze. Life can't get any better than this.

I look over at Ilene. She's given up counting honeymooners and is lying flat on the other fender counting stars. "Six and seven and eight and nine," she counts out loud. Quickly I lie back and start counting stars, too. If I hurry I can catch up with her.

"One, two, three, four, five," I count.

1942

Sam Katz and I are necking in the living room. We have waited a long time. Not to neck. To neck in the living room.

My sisters and I have unwritten rules in our house. These rules were never decreed, but just fell into place. Dina and her boyfriend get the living room. Ilene and her steady, Al Katz, Sam's older brother, get the sun parlor. Which leaves the kitchen for me and my dates. When one sister is away or doesn't have a date we all move up a peg. Once in awhile, I luck out and get the living room. That's what happened tonight.

Sam and I were just hanging out with friends tonight and got home early. Neither Dina nor Ilene is home; thus our windfall. On the radio Glen Miller is softly playing, "The Nearness of You." The only light is coming through the French doors from the hall. In the distance we sometimes hear Mom and Dad upstairs in bed, rustling the pages of the newspaper. All is going blissfully. This is a lot more romantic than necking in the kitchen.

Soon we hear the back door slam. It's Ilene and Al.

"Darn," Sam says, "time to play musical rooms." It's hard to give up this luxury, even to a relative.

Ilene and Al enter the living room prepared to take their rightful place in the pecking order.

Sam stalls for time. "What did you see, that Lou Gehrig movie?" he asks.

"Uh huh. 'Pride of the Yankees,'" his brother supplies.

"How was it?"

Al doesn't answer but I see him give Sam a look that says, "O.K., out."

I don't know why Ilene and Al need privacy. They have been going steady for over three years. They've never been the least bit shy about showing their affection in public. They don't wait for the living room or even the sun parlor to neck. As far as I can see they neck all the time they're together.

"I think your hugging and kissing in public is terrible," I've told Ilene many times over the years. She doesn't listen.

Ilene and I never really met the Katz brothers. We have always known each other. Ilene tells this story when people ask how she and Al met. "One afternoon," she relates, "Goldie Katz came to visit my Mom, who had just had a baby. Goldie put her six month old baby in the crib next to Mom's. That's how Al and I met, in bed."

Unlike Ilene and Al, Sam and I started to feel romantic about each other just a few months ago. I have my new haircut to thank. For the first time since I was a kid I have bangs. One look at the new me and Sam was mine. Maybe he has a hair fetish. That's all right, too. I'll never be without bangs again.

I never told anyone except my diary, but when I was ten or twelve I had a big crush on Sam. "Sam Katz skated with me at the rink today. I really like him. Some day I bet he'll be my boyfriend. Maybe I'll marry him." A few weeks later I wrote, "Went to the skating rink today. Sam Katz wasn't there. Darn."

I got over my crush years before we got to high school. Sam and I became confidantes and good friends. We were in the same crowd and often dated each other's best friends. The only time we dated each other was when my Dad laid down the law.

When Dina was growing up, she was not allowed to date non-Jewish boys. With Ilene, Dad was somewhat more lenient. She occasionally managed to sneak a few gentiles past Dad, but not often. By the time I was dating, Dad spent a lot of time looking the other way. Poor Dad, I guess three daughters were just one more than he could handle.

Once in awhile, probably spurred on by reports of intermarriage that came to his attention, Dad would go on a rampage. Somehow it always seemed to be when my high school sorority was having a dance. "You can't go unless you go with a Jewish boy," my Father would decree. More often than not, that "Jewish boy" would be Sam Katz. There wasn't a large roster of Jewish males to pick from in Niagara Falls. It was all right, though. Sam and I always had a good time together and as soon as Dad's crisis had passed I would go back to dating Chet Cleveland or Bill Murphy or Jack Burns.

I hear a cheery, "Hi, we're home." Dina and her boyfriend obviously had a great time tonight. They flop onto the living room sofa. Without a word spoken, Ilene and Al drift toward the sun parlor, Sam and I head for the kitchen.

No one even has time to settle in. Suddenly, the hall light flashes on and off. Once, twice, three times. That is the infamous Nimelman signal. Whenever Dad decides that it's time for all visiting males to leave the premises he flicks the light on and off in the upstairs hall, which also controls the downstairs hall light. Three flicks have a special meaning. They signal, "And I do mean now."

"But we just got here," Al mutters angrily.

"We just walked in the door," moans Dina. Her boyfriend looks miffed, too.

After quick goodnight kisses, three males hurry out into the night. Two of them are disgruntled and mumbling, but Sam Katz got to neck in the comfort of the living room tonight. He's smiling.

1969

"Remember everything," Ilene admonishes for the tenth time. "I want to hear all the details."

Ilene, Al, Sam and I are in the middle of dinner. Tomorrow morning we will all go to the Los Angeles airport. Ilene and Al will catch a flight back to Buffalo after their annual week's visit with us. Sam and I will set out on an exciting weekend in Las Vegas.

We are going to be the guests of Sammy Davis, Sr. at a birthday party for his son, Sammy Jr. Sammy Sr. and his wife, whom everyone calls Pee Wee, left for Vegas today and will be waiting for us when we arrive tomorrow.

We met the Davis' at a party several months ago and have become friends. When they invited us to join them at the birthday celebration we jumped at the chance. Last night we had a few couples over and Ilene and Al met Pee Wee and Sammy Sr., too. Sammy enjoys talking about his Will Maston Trio days as much as everyone enjoys hearing about them. Last night he had been in rare form and kept us all entertained with his show biz reminiscing.

The phone rings. Sam bounces up from the dinner table to answer. He listens intently for a long time. We all stop eating to watch his ever changing expression. Finally we hear, "Hold the line a minute, Sammy. I'll find out." Turning to us, he explains, "Sammy made a mistake, the party is scheduled for tonight. He says there's a plane out every hour. We can hop the next one and get there in plenty of time. The party doesn't start till after the last show.

"And," Sam draws out, "he wants to know if you (indicating Ilene and Al) would like to detour through Vegas on your way home and come to the party, too." Ilene's theatrical swoon on the dining room floor is all the answer he needs. From that moment until we land in Las Vegas Ilene and Al don't stop grinning.

Just as Sammy predicted, we arrive in plenty of time. The room is chock full of celebrities and almost celebrities. It looks, sounds, and feels like New Year's Eve.

"Don't you feel like we're Alice and Alex in Wonderland?" I whisper to Sam as we walk down the long corridor to the ballroom. I turn to speak to Ilene and Al, who I thought were right behind us, and come face to face with a woman stunningly swathed in a black Russian Cossack-like wool suit complete with tall Persian lamb hat and muff to match. It's Barbra Streisand! She skirts us and I see Ilene and Al tittering at my confusion.

The four of us take up positions in the middle of the ballroom. Had we still been kids we would have gawked, squealed, and pointed. Being sophisticated adults, we stand, cocktail glasses in hand, sneaking sidelong glances, surreptitiously nudging each other, and pretending to be deep in conversation while scanning the room over each other's shoulders.

"No one can tell me half the people in this room aren't doing the same thing," Sam declares. "They just have more finesse than we. They've had more practice."

Cocktails consumed, the guests are asked to be seated for dinner. Sammy Sr. and PeeWee lead the way to our table. We are seated with Sammy Jr.'s orchestra leader, Bill Rhodes, his wife, and a few other familiar faces. Ilene and I make eye contact. She rolls her eyes. I laugh and wink.

Sammy Jr. and his wife, Altovese, stop by our table.

"Happy birthday, Sammy," we greet.

Two drinks have convinced us that we are on a first name basis.

"Thank you for coming," he replies, flashing his famous grin at the four of us. In quick succession Mel Torme, Buddy Hackett, and Marty Allen stop by to greet Sammy Sr. and are introduced. We progress rapidly from a polite "Nice to meet you, Mr. Torme," to "Hi, Buddy," to "Hey, what's happenin', Marty?"

"This is great!" the four of us agree when we have a moment alone, "We could get used to this life."

Stardust fills our eyes.

Suddenly, Sammy Sr. says, "Come on, Ethyl, I'll introduce you to Barbra." He indicates Sammy Jr.'s group two tables away where Streisand is holding court.

"No, Sammy," I reply, "I already ran into her. She's busy over there. I don't have to meet her. She won't remember, anyway."

Sammy has had at least as much to drink as we. The more I resist, the more he insists. It becomes embarrassing.

"O.K., Sammy," I finally relent. He leads me to his son's table. Sammy Jr. pauses in his conversation with a vaguely familiar face, nods, and smiles. Sammy Sr. approaches Barbra with me in tow.

"Barbra," he begins over the din, "I want you to meet my friend, Ethyl Katz."

"How do you do," I say, wishing that I had a more exotic name.

Barbra looks straight ahead. Not only does she not acknowledge me, she doesn't even turn to look at Sammy. Seconds that seem like minutes pass. Mortification immobilizes me. Finally I hear a barely audible, "How do you do."

Sneaking a peek around to see if anyone has witnessed my humiliation, I slink back to our table. Unaware of my absence, Ilene, Al and Sam are still bouncing along on the cloud from which I have just fallen. They are trading repartee with Buddy Hackett and Mel Torme. Every few seconds they all burst into loud guffaws.

"Aren't they a riot?" Ilene asks merrily.

"They're just people," I reply grumpily.

1984

It is 11:15. A cool May evening. Sam is in the bedroom going through the get-ready-for-bed ritual. Normally I would be there, too, watching the eleven o'clock news on TV while washing and brushing and all. But tonight I want to spend some time alone with my sister, so I don't follow him into the bedroom. Sam says nothing, but I sense that he understands.

I put the matches and candle I am holding on the dining room table and slouch comfortably into one of the dining room chairs.

"OK, Ilene," I say, "Sam's gone to bed. I went first last time, so it's your turn now."

A long pause. I wait.

"OK, here's one," Ilene says, already laughing. "It must have been just a few years after both of us married, and, Ethyl, I'll never forget your voice on the phone:

"Ilene, I just got a phone call from a crazy lady. She says she found my phone number written on a matchbox her husband left on the dresser. She says she knows I'm having an affair with him and I better stop. Ilene, I don't even recognize the name."

"Oh cool it, Ethyl, I told you, 'I just got the same call and I've figured out that Romeo is the guy who's painting our houses. He probably wrote our names and numbers on a match box when he was painting Rosalie's house and she told him we'd like him to call us about painting our houses, too.'"

Ilene and I start to laugh now, remembering what he looked like. Unshaven, an undershirt that never quite covered his rotund belly, and pants that started just below that exposed bit of anatomy.

Ilene wipes her eyes and turns to me still laughing. "O.K. Now it's your turn."

"This one happened not too long after that," I begin. "I answer the phone and there's a man's voice."

"Is this the Katz residence?"

"Yes, it is."

"Is this the Katz who's in the Naval Reserve?"

"Yes, but his brother is, too. Are you looking for my husband, Sam, or for his brother, Al?"

"I don't know the first name, but he's in the insurance business."

"My husband is, but Al is, too."

"He's married to a Nimelman girl."

"Yes, that's me, but my sister is married to Sam's brother, so it's her, too."

"She' a teacher."

"I am, but she is, too."

"She teaches art at Gaskill Jr. High."

"Oh, you're looking for Al and Ilene. Here's their number."

Ilene's smile is wistful now.

"God, that was over thirty years ago," she sighs. "Our lives were like a duet, weren't they?"

"Yes," I reply. After a pause I add, "You know, it's hard to believe. Is it really five years that you've been gone?"

We sit in silence for a long time—until I don't feel her anymore.

I strike a match, light the candle in the glass, and whisper the mourner's prayer. "Yisgedal," I pray, "yisgedash...."

1945

"You're getting red, turn over," I command.

Ilene opens one eye. "Red? I'm too tan to burn."

"Trust me, you're red," I reply.

Ilene sits up on the towel, dusts the sand from her hands, and slathers more suntan oil on her arms and legs.

I squint at the swishing palm fronds high above and inhale the sweet smell of coconut oil. "Sure is a strange way to spend our honeymoons," I muse.

"Yeah," Ilene replies.

It had never entered our minds three short weeks ago, when Sam came home on leave, that within two weeks we would be wed. We had already made the decision. We'd wait until the war was over to marry. By that time I'd be out of school and working while Sam finished his interrupted education. Unlike Ilene and Al, we'd be practical. It was definite—until Sam received an offer from the United States Navy that we couldn't refuse.

Al and Ilene married a month ago, as soon as Al's officer's training was over. He's stationed at the Navy base in Miami, Florida. They live in Miami Beach. Sam completed officer's training school a week ago and he came home on leave to await further orders. Those orders came yesterday. Of all the places in the world he could have been assigned, he, too, was ordered to report for duty to the Navy base in Miami.

We called Ilene and Al. The four of us agreed that this was too good to pass up. It was meant to be.

That's why, although Ilene and I spend our evenings with our new husbands, we spend our honeymoon afternoons lolling on the beach. Alone together.

Assemblage II

"And the sun fell warm upon his face like a hand with a lovely touch."

The Secret Garden

Prologue

The early morning air is moist, the sun already warm. At Giverney in Monet's country garden I pause and sink onto a worn wooden bench half-hidden by flowering azalea bushes. I survey the sparkling pond, its graceful bridge, the fragrant flowers. The insects buzzing about their daily chores in the pink azaleas hum a tune to me and I supply the lyrics:

Shielded by the sturdy oak and watched over by the whispering willow, snug in our garden, we matured. Jaunty, drooping, sturdy, delicate, season after season we pushed towards the sun. Sometimes over-watered, sometimes parched, it made no difference. We flourished.

The weather was kind, buffeting us more than some, but less than most. By the time the sturdy oak was felled and the willow withered, we flowers were deeply rooted and could make it on our own.

Then tragedy struck. Without warning, insidious tentacles of crabgrass encircled the most brilliant flower of all and tightened its relentless grip. Borne on a gentle wind, the withered flower disappeared, and all remaining were left to contemplate the scarred soil where once it had so gracefully held sway.

The mulching leaves of passing seasons have now softened the scar and what remains is a mound of rich, dark earth that nourishes and strengthens the clumps of blossoms and buds that have closed ranks around it.

Something tickles my arm. Instinctively, I brush it away. A beautiful red ladybug tumbles to the bench beside me. I smile down at it. It moves a little closer. It knows I meant no harm.

1954

Enough of this self-pity, I chide myself. Stop dwelling on what might have been. He's been gone only four days so far.

Sam and I really got excited two weeks ago when word came down that this year his Naval Reserve Squadron would be based in Memphis for their two weeks of maneuvers. This was the first time that the tour of duty was on land. Usually they were aboard aircraft carriers or other ships. Land meant that I could fly down and be with him for at least part of the two weeks.

Our excitement was short lived. We never dreamed the airfare from Buffalo to Memphis was so expensive. With that, the hotel room, and everything else, the trip was just too costly. So Sam is in Memphis, and I am home.

I pick up the phone to call Ilene, although she's no barrel of laughs these days, either. Sam and Al are in the same squadron, so they're in Memphis together.

Ilene's voice is actually chipper.

"Ethyl, I was about to call you. Quick, get the paper. Look at page twelve."

She holds while I follow her instructions. A full-page ad by Eastern Airlines announces a discount fare, effective immediately. "Any child under eighteen can fly free if accompanied by a parent." It's the answer to our prayers.

Hallelujah! So we're sisters! So we're only eighteen months apart! So we're both over thirty! Minor obstacles.

Three days later Ilene and I are walking down the long concourse at the Buffalo airport. We're nervous wrecks. We're also a sorry sight.

Ilene has pulled back her long blonde hair and pinned it into a donut at the nape of her neck. Atop it she has plopped a black straw hat with a long feather that sticks straight up. It elongates her five foot six stature, making the actual two inch difference in our heights appear even greater. Ilene, who is amply endowed, has loosened her bra straps below and beyond the call of duty. A nice matronly touch. A white collar held by a cameo brooch peeks from under her severe black suit. Service weight hose and black oxfords complete her outfit.

I skip along at her side in my bobby socks and saddle shoes. She stands erect; I slouch. My blonde-streaked brunette hair is hidden under a flowered bandanna, which is tied under my chin. I wear my high school sorority pin on my sloppy pullover sweater and a plaid pleated skirt. To complete what we hope is the illusion I carry a geometry textbook.

As we nervously thread our way to Gate 8, Ilene whispers to me, "If we see anyone we know I'll absolutely die right on the spot." So, naturally, we come face to face with Phil Gellman, a friend and promising young attorney in Niagara Falls. Ilene is stronger than she thinks. We exchange as few pleasantries as necessary and move on.

He didn't even flinch at our appearance. How insulting.

We have agreed that Ilene will do all the talking. She checks us in at the gate.

"My daughter and I are going to Memphis," she says. "This is the right gate, isn't it?"

My heart is pounding so loud I'm afraid the man behind the counter can hear it. He eyes us for a long moment. Is he suspicious or just noting silently that nerdy mothers beget nerdy kids? Without a word he hands Ilene our tickets, turns from us, and calls, "Next."

Ilene and I sink into our seats aboard the plane. She sits in the aisle seat and calls me "dear." I keep my face buried in the geometry book and call her "mom."

The stewardess starts counting passengers. She stops at our side, facing us. I feel faint, then notice that she is just letting a passenger squeeze by. She bumps Ilene's arm, says, "Excuse me," and continues her head count.

Five hours later, as our plane hovers over Memphis, I whisper to Ilene, "Do you realize we have to do this all over again going home?" We feign horror and giggle.

As we exit the plane we see our husbands standing there waiting for us. They look oh-so-handsome in their Naval officer uniforms. We sprint to them and literally jump into their waiting arms.

1933

We have a sun parlor in our house. It goes across the whole front of the house and has windows all across three sides. Every side except the one that backs up to the living room. All the windows have six panes in the top half and six in the bottom. Mom says it makes them hard to wash, but they do look cozy.

Mom has tall rubber plants in the room. I guess the sun and air in there are just right for rubber plants because they get so tall she has to cut off the tops when they reach the ceiling. She starts a new plant with what she cuts off and pretty soon the new plant is as tall as its mother. Just when it starts looking like a jungle instead of a garden in there Mom gives some of the rubber plants to her friends. They are very grateful. So are Ilene and I. We were beginning to feel crowded in there. We are the only ones who ever use the sun parlor.

Almost every afternoon, we go there, just the two of us. There's a big wicker sofa in there and an armchair to match. They're not at all like anyone else's furniture. Instead of getting them in white or wood color like everyone else, Mom got dark green wicker. The cushions are all covered with huge pink roses, light and dark. Mom calls them cabbage roses. A little green shows, but no stems. It's like being high up and looking down at the faces of a garden full of flowers.

Even though there is the big sofa, that isn't where we usually sit. We sit together in the wicker chair. Sometimes Ilene draws pictures for me that look like a comic strip. She tells me a story as she draws. It's almost always about a girl who works in a big office, has lots of boyfriends, and wears beautiful clothes. It reminds me of "Tillie the Toiler" on the comic page in the paper. I think that's where Ilene gets her ideas, except that Ilene's girls, who are almost always named Nancy, wear wonderful dresses and gowns that Ilene designs for them right on the spot. They always marry the boss's son.

Sometimes, instead of comic strips, Ilene and I sit in the chair and read a book. Ilene knows more words than I do, so she reads most of the time. She keeps her place with her finger, and when she comes to words that I have had or ones she thinks I can sound out, she keeps quiet and lets me read.

Right now we're reading a wonderful book. It's called *The Secret Garden*. It's all about a girl named Mary, and her magical friend, Dickon, and her sick cousin, Colin, who's really not sick at all.

Ilene is pointing. I am reading:

"And it was like that with Colin when he first saw and heard and felt the Springtime inside the four high walls of a hidden garden. That afternoon the whole world seemed to devote itself to being perfect and radiantly beautiful and kind to one boy. Perhaps out of pure heavenly goodness the spring came and crowded everything it possibly could into that one place. More than once Dickon paused in what he was doing and stood still with a sort of growing wonder in his eyes, shaking his head softly."

"You read the whole paragraph all by yourself," Ilene cheers. Ilene really helped me, but just once, with the word "radiantly."

I'm excited. I feel like a genius. I look ahead on the page. There seem to be a lot of strange words. Luckily, Mom's voice calls from the kitchen. "Ilene, Ethyl, get cleaned up. Dinner's almost ready."

Ilene marks our place and closes the book.

Outside the windows the sun is low in the sky now. It shines on the sparkly snow that is stuck to the windowpanes. The room is filled with a gold light so bright that it hurts my eyes. Ilene and I look around at Mom's wicker sofa all filled with huge cabbage roses and her rubber plants that reach way up to the ceiling. Everything looks so beautiful in that strange gold light. It makes me want to cry.

"It's magic," I whisper.

"It's our own secret garden," Ilene whispers back.

For no reason at all, we tiptoe out of the room to get ready for dinner.

1946

What's the matter with me? Here I sit, pen in hand, staring at these darn application forms for teaching jobs. Why am I having such a hard time getting started?

It's July. I'm in my final quarter at the University of Buffalo where I transferred after my freshman year at Ohio State. In August I'll be qualified to teach commercial subjects in high school. Sam's a sophomore at Niagara University. He returned from Guam and got his Navy discharge just in time to enroll for the summer session.

We've been married almost a year, and now that the war is over we are settling down, getting on with our lives. With both of us in college there are financial problems, but who cares? Come Fall, I'll be teaching. We'll have it made then. That is, if I ever get these applications filled out. What is my problem? It isn't as if I haven't worked before. Since I was fifteen, I've held various jobs and that doesn't include the days in Mom and Dad's grocery store.

I laugh, thinking of that very first job eight years ago. I can see sixteen-year-old Ilene returning home from her Saturday job working in Stewart's Dress Shop on Main Street.

"Ethyl, I have great news," she announces. "They need more Saturday sales help at the store. I told the manager about you. If you can get working papers and a social security number by next Friday she'll hire you."

I cannot believe my luck. I'm just fifteen. My only experience is helping in Dad's grocery store and here I am hired, sight unseen. A shop on Main Street, no less. Ilene must have done some promotion job.

Unlike most shops on Main Street, where dresses cost anywhere from $19.95 up, in Stewart's they are all $7.95 and down. Even with this advantage, my first venture into the business world turns out to be a disaster. It seems I lack sales ability. Ilene comes to my rescue. Several times each Saturday, she writes my name on her sales slips. It makes me look good and saves my job.

As luck would have it, within six months, Stewart's goes out of business. I feel a little guilty.

I ease into retirement. Ilene gets another Saturday job at Lerner's.

Within weeks she again arrives home with news. "Mr. White at Thom McAn's shoe store next door needs someone to sell purses. I told him about you. He wants to see you."

Why not, I tell myself. I should pull my own weight. It's not bad getting five dollars for just one day's work.

Thankfully, I am much better at selling purses than I was at selling dresses. I choose to believe that at sixteen I've gained credibility.

Ilene, however, is not finished managing my career.

"Art Gray needs an extra cashier during the Christmas rush," she informs me one day.

Art Gray has a children's shoe store.

"I'm working full-time at Lerner's during the vacation," she continues, "but I told him that you probably have some days available. He said he would call you."

He does call and I do work.

Now Mr. White and Art Gray vie for my Saturdays each week. It's flattering, but this is getting to be much too time consuming. Everyone needs a social life.

"You can stop any time now," I tell Ilene, only half joking.

Time passes. Ilene is still going steady with Al Katz.

One day she announces, "I was talking to Al's mother today. She needs help in her store."

Mrs. Katz is a milliner and, I understand, a hard taskmaster.

"You didn't recommend me, did you?" I ask.

"No," Ilene answers. "I just told her that if I were staying at the University of Buffalo I would have been happy to help her out, but since I'll be leaving for Ohio State soon, I can't. And I just kinda mentioned," she adds innocently, "that once in awhile you have Saturday free."

I now have three employers. Ilene goes away to school.

Two years later Ilene graduates from Ohio State. The following Fall I enroll. Unfortunately, Ilene taught Sunday School while there. I've hardly had time to unpack and settle in when a call comes from the Sunday School director. "We liked Ilene so much," he flatters. "Would you be interested?"

Of course I take the job. How can I not? It wouldn't be right. Between Ilene's strong work ethic and my strong guilt complex, I'm doomed.

My eyes focus again on the stack of job applications in front of me. No more daydreaming. I've got to get this done. I've had loads of jobs, I've just never applied for one. No wonder applying for a teaching job seems so formidable. I tackle the pile of application forms.

I'm still poring over them when the telephone rings. It's Ilene. "Ethyl, I just had a teaching interview with the principal at Lewiston High School," she tells me. "It turns out they don't need an art teacher, so that leaves me out," she continues, "but he's desperately searching for someone to teach typing, bookkeeping, and all those other business subjects. He nearly kissed me when I told him about you."

I take the job and gladly throw the whole pile of application blanks into the trash.

Ilene gets pregnant and is no longer involved in job hunting, for her or for me. Finally, I sigh, I am free of Ilene's ambition.

Three blissful months pass.

It's a balmy October evening. Sam is studying and I am correcting papers. The phone rings. Sam out waits me and I pick up the phone to hear Ilene's voice. "Guess what I just heard?" she asks excitedly. "Niagara Falls Adult Education needs a typing and shorthand teacher. It's only two nights a week. Just right for you, and—"

1938

I stand straight and tall at the altar. Here goes, I think. My big ending and then I can sit down.

My heart pounds but I try to look serene. I glance beside me at Rabbi Porrath. He is sitting in a big red velvet armchair wearing his white robe, skullcap, and tallis. He looks the way I picture God would look if he were human. I look down at the congregants. They seem to be hanging on my every word.

"The grass withereth," I intone in a whisper. A gentle smile turns up the corners of my mouth, just as I had practiced it.

My voice gets louder and more intense. "The flowers fadeth." I pause for effect.

Now for the grand finale, a mighty pronouncement that will bounce off the sanctuary walls and stun the audience. "But the word of God shall stand forever." It's not quite as loud and dramatic as I had planned but passable. I take my seat on the podium. I have fulfilled the Nimelman legacy. Dina, Ilene, and I have each delivered the coveted floral offering at our respective confirmations. The rest of the confirmation ceremony passes in a haze.

When we finally spot each other at the reception in the vestry, Ilene wends her way through the crowd to my side. I wait for her critique. "You were great, really great," she tells me, "but I would have delivered the ending the way that I told you I did it, loud and forceful throughout. I think it was more effective that way."

"Maybe, but I wanted mine to be different," I answer truthfully.

"I see," Ilene says. And I think she really does.

1935

Can you believe it? Ilene is thirteen and I'm eleven and we still have to go to bed by 8:30. What a pain. But not tonight. Tonight we have a plan.

Ilene and I have a secret. A really big secret we have never told anyone.

We spy on the parties Mom and Dad have in the living room downstairs. We lie on our stomachs in the dark upstairs hall. We press our heads against the banisters of the winding staircase and listen to everything that is going on in the living room. We can even see a little of the living room through the big doors that separate it from the downstairs hall.

Now, about our plan. At dinner tonight Mom had said to Dad, "A few of the girls are coming over tonight while you fellows are at your meeting." Ilene and I had sneaked peeks at each other. We read each other's minds that way.

It's nine o'clock now. Mom's friends are jabbering away. Ilene and I have been in bed for almost half an hour already. Across the narrow space between our twin beds I whisper, "OK, Ilene, the coast is clear."

No answer.

"Ilene, it's time!"

No answer. She's asleep! Darn! Well, I'll just have to do it myself and tell my sister about it in the morning.

I take up my station in the hall. My head is pressed so tight against the banister that it hurts. It's my first solo spying and I don't want to mess up.

Mrs. Monkarsh is talking. "I'm not the least bit surprised that Dina was picked for AZA sweetheart," she says.

Dina is a teenager. She has her own room and acts so grown up it's disgusting.

Mrs. Monkarsh continues, "I think she's the prettiest girl in the whole school." All the women seem to agree because I hear, "She has eyes like Betty Boop", and "She's a little kewpie doll." And lots, lots more.

Now Mrs. Passer's voice. "As beautiful as Dina is, as far as I'm concerned, Ilene is the stunner." Quickly I think, if Dina is a kewpie doll and Ilene a stunner, I can hardly wait till they get to me. Mrs. Passer again, "That pretty blond hair and those green eyes, I'm telling you, that Ilene is a stunner."

Wow, I think, a stunner twice! But now it's my turn. I'm the only sister left. Now they'll talk about me.

At last I hear good old Aunt Goldie, "And that Ethyl, what a great kid."

Mrs. Passer interrupts as if Aunt Goldie hasn't even spoken. "You mark my word. Someday Ilene will even outshine Dina. She'll be the real family beauty."

Great kid? Great kid! It keeps ringing in my ears. I don't want to be a great kid. I want someone to call me pretty. Mrs. Passer, Mrs. Monkarsh, what about me? I want to be pretty, too.

My sobs are so loud I'm afraid that they'll hear me. I fall into bed and press my face into the pillow so Ilene can't hear me cry.

It's morning. Ilene is leaning over me. Her stupid, pretty blond hair tickles my nose, and I remember.

"Ethyl," she says, "We fell asleep and forgot to spy."

I just shrug. It's the very first time in my whole life that I have a secret I can't even tell Ilene.

Assemblage III

"I will pat your hand and stroke it and sing something quite low."

The Secret Garden

Prologue

The late afternoon sun slants through the glass doors, creating a wide shaft that cuts through the cool, shaded family room. Dust particles bounce about in the bright ribbon of light. My gaze is caught by one speck. I follow its progress as it twists and turns, bumping its fellow dancers. It finally whirls away and gets lost in the crowd.

In the slanted rays of light I see Ilene's hospital room. Ilene is weak. Her tongue is thick. I stand at the foot of her bed as she whispers a personal message to each member of the family. Sometimes the listener looks puzzled. I repeat her words. My ears don't always know, but I do. I understand each word. "Is that what you are saying, Ilene?" I ask. She nods.

Sometimes she is direct. Sometimes she makes oblique references. The person she is speaking to is confused and turns to me to ask, "Why is she telling me that?" I interpret, explaining the meaning. Each time I ask, "Is that right, Ilene?" Each time she nods.

The sun passes behind a cloud. The bright ribbon of light disappears. The dust dancers are gone. So is Ilene.

1949

It is standard procedure. At least it is in Niagara Falls. Two years after marriage, the wife gets pregnant. By the third anniversary, the little darling is firmly ensconced in his or her own little domain. Almost all of my friends have adhered to the schedule. So did Ilene. Dina was a bit behind schedule. I think she had trouble conceiving. Dina's Suzy and Ilene's Terri are just seventeen days apart. They are two years old now.

What a joy it's been to watch them grow. Suzy got a tooth soon after birth. Terri was found one morning leaning precariously out of her crib. No one dreamed she would be standing so soon.

Sam and I have been married four years, but we don't have a child yet. Not that we haven't wanted one. The time hasn't been right. That is, not until six months ago.

We were married almost a year when Sam got out of the Navy. Shortly after that I was graduated from UB. For several years I taught while Sam finished at Niagara University. Six months ago, when he graduated, we rejoiced. "The time is now," we told each other. We soon found that begetting a child was more easily planned than accomplished.

It has been difficult waiting this long for parenthood. These last six months feel like six years to us. More than once I've overheard my friends' parents ask them, "How come the Katzes don't have a baby? They've been married four years." I see my friends trying to shush their inquisitive parents. They look over at us to see if we've heard. I feel like saying, "We've been trying! Any suggestions?"

It's sunny and warm today. I take a walk and stop by at Ilene's house on Porter Road. Rosy cheeked Terri is just up from her nap. I roll a fabric ball to her. She picks it up and throws it back in my general direction. Then we repeat the process. Ilene is watching us. I try to sound off-handed but avoid looking at her.

"Another month, and I'm still not pregnant," I tell her.

Ilene doesn't answer.

I glance over. Tears are rolling down her face.

I feel terrible.

"It's O.K., Ilene. Maybe I'll get pregnant next month."

Ilene's tears continue.

"I am," she says.

"Am what? Pregnant?" I ask.

Ilene nods.

"Don't you want to be?" I'm amazed.

"Of course I do. But not before you," she answers.

I end up consoling Ilene—because I'm not pregnant!

Unfortunately, two months later, Ilene has a miscarriage.

Three more months pass and, finally, Sam and I think we've conceived. It seems too good to be true. Difficult as it is, Sam and I wait to tell until we are certain. Within two weeks I get queasy and go nowhere without the nauseated expectant mother's best friend, Nabisco soda crackers.

It's a Friday evening. Sam and I pick up Ilene to go to Buffalo. Al is working in Buffalo and will meet us there. Ilene gets in the front seat with us.

"Hi, what's new?" she greets us.

"Not much," we lie. "What's doing with you? How's Terri?"

Ilene begins to relate Terri's latest antic.

I reach for the box of soda crackers that is wedged on the seat between Sam and me and start munching on one. I watch Ilene out of the corner of my eye. She stops in mid-sentence, gapes, and bursts into tears. This time I join her.

1932

What is that tapping on the window?

Ilene is asleep in the other twin bed. She doesn't even know we're in danger. If I can just get over to her bed she'll protect me 'cause she's ten. I'm only nine.

But it's the second floor!

So what? Didn't the kidnapper use a stepladder to get to that Lindbergh baby? It's him, I know it's him! I crouch under my blankets. My heart is pounding so hard I can hear it.

I dare a quick peek at the window. It's dark. I see nothing. All I hear is the wind howling through the bare tree branches. I make my move. With one sudden leap I am in my sister's bed, scrambling under her blankets. She stirs a little and moves to make room for me. I cuddle close to her.

You know, I bet it was just the wind. My eyes get heavy.

I've got to go. What do I do now? I've really got to go! No, sir, not me. I'm not going anywhere! What if the kidnapper comes back? I am not taking one step out of this bed! I cuddle closer to Ilene and doze off.

I wake with a start. Ilene is fast asleep beside me and I've just wet her bed! It's almost morning. I can just make out the shapes of the bed and dresser. I slip quietly back into my own bed. Ilene will never even know I was there.

I doze again. What a night.

Suddenly, my Father's voice says, "What do you mean you didn't even feel it? You're ten years old, Ilene, you are not a baby."

Ilene is crying. I keep my eyes closed and make believe I'm still sleeping. Dad leaves the room. From the direction of my sister's bed a heavy object hits my back. I think it's a shoe. But I don't move.

1990

"That is not the criterion," my niece Terri says, a slight edge creeping into her voice.

Startled, I look up from the design I've been etching with my fingernail into the frost on the tall glass in front of me. The similarities are all there just as I remember them—the frown, the narrowed eyes, the pursed lips all precursors of a gathering squall.

Terri sees me staring at her. The frown disappears, her eyes clear, the dark clouds pass. "That is not the criterion," she repeats more gently.

Terri and I are seated at the most secluded table we were able to find in the coffee shop at the Buffalo airport. We are sipping cokes and discussing the primary reason for my just completed three day stay, a gallery opening of Terri's latest series of paintings. My plane back to Los Angeles leaves in an hour.

It has been exciting though hectic. Having these few minutes alone with Terri is a special treat even though, at the moment, we are having a philosophical argument.

I have made the mistake of confessing my joy when, at one point during the opening, I had surreptitiously counted the red dots beside paintings and found that at least half of the paintings had already been purchased.

"The criterion of a successful show is how well it's received by the public in general and art mavens in particular," she says, "not how many pieces are sold."

"O.K.," I argue, "then what you are saying is that if every person who was there, from the director of Albright Knox to the fellow parking cars, really loved the show, but not one piece was purchased, you would have considered the show a success."

"Yes," Terri declares emphatically.

Another habit she inherited, I think.

"A likely story," I reply.

We both laugh and our conversation meanders along other paths until my flight is announced.

After a tearful farewell, I settle into my aisle seat and am pleased to note the empty seat next to mine and the man near the window who is already leafing through a notebook. Good, no one with whom I am obligated to exchange pleasantries.

I endure my usual routine, a white-knuckle takeoff and an anxious few minutes of buffeting as we climb through clouds to our assigned slot in the sky. "Cruising altitude, and clear skies all the way into Los Angeles," the Captain finally announces.

"Good work," I mutter as I relinquish my copilot duties to the man American Airlines pays to do the job.

I relax. My eyes close.

"Of course I knew it, Ilene," I hear myself saying. "I didn't see you, but as soon as I walked into the Gallery I felt your presence. It was a good feeling knowing you were there. But God forbid you should speak to me."

That's right, Ilene giggles, He did.

"You're very funny," I frown, then I giggle too.

We babble on, proud mother and aunt discussing the strength and depth in Terri's latest work.

"I don't see how she can top it," I conclude. "I feel that this series is not just a step forward for her, but a giant leap, don't you?" I ask.

Ilene nods.

"And," I blithely continue, "did you know that more than half of the paintings were purchased that very first night?"

A slight edge creeps into Ilene's voice. She frowns, her eyes narrow, her lips purse. That is not the criterion of a successful show, she answers huffily.

"Right," I answer, and am actually relieved to feel a hand on my shoulder and hear a voice ask, "Would you like chicken or fish for your entree, ma'am?"

1980

Although Sam and I moved into our new condo at the beach a week ago, this is the first time I've taken a break from unpacking to try the outdoor amenities the real estate agent had so enthusiastically touted. I approach the jacuzzi and gingerly stick my big toe into the seething inferno. There are two women soaking in the frothy bubbles.

"You can't do it by inches," the redhead volunteers, "take the plunge. It only hurts for a second."

I take her advice and sink into the steaming whirlpool until all that shows above the churning suds is my head. Introductions ensue followed by the usual investigative chitchat, where we each lived before, when and why we moved.

The timer switches off the jets but no one makes a move to leave the pool. This is fun.

"Did you know each other before coming here?" I ask.

They look at each other and laugh.

The redhead answers, "Didn't we tell you? We're sisters."

Sisters! My vision blurs. I scoop up hot water with my cupped hands and splash it into my face. It doesn't help.

"Got to get back to work," I mumble and hoist myself awkwardly out of the pool. I gather up my belongings and hurry to the privacy of our apartment.

Closing the door behind me, I sniffle away the tears. Slowly it comes into focus. The tall rubber plants…the green wicker sofa and matching chair…the small rectangular windowpanes and the strange golden light.

All is quiet.

Please come, Ilene. I've got to talk to you.

Silence.

Remember, Ilene? In the hospital that day? You promised! You said, "We'll meet in our secret garden." That's what you said.

I wait. Nothing happens.

Where are you, Ilene? I can feel the anger rising in my chest. You promised we'd meet here in our secret garden. This isn't the first time I've come looking for you. You never appear. I've felt your presence other places but never here. Never when I needed you. It has always been when you felt like it. Why do you always have to be in charge? Knowing you'd meet me here whenever I needed you was the only thing that made your going bearable. Why did you promise if you didn't mean it?

I stop ranting. What have I done? She may never come again. Not here, not anywhere.

I hurry to apologize. I'm sorry. I'm sure you have your reasons. We'll do it your way. Wherever and whenever you want. Just don't stop coming at all. O.K?

Still no answer.

I walk into the bathroom and splash cold water on my face. Don't worry, I assure the image in the mirror. She'll understand. Everything will be fine.

1958

"You're so stubborn," Ilene admonishes. "Try it just this once."

She has stopped by my house on her way home from her weekly art class. My sister has studied art since she was a kid and is very talented.

A number of years ago Ilene decided that I have what she calls "latent artistic ability."

In her more dramatic moments she accuses me directly, "You, Ethyl, are not living up to your potential."

I've been hearing this for five years now.

"Where has this great talent been hiding?" I ask her. "I didn't have it when I was in school."

Usually, Ilene just makes a face. This time she ignores me and silently walks around my house gathering props. A bowl here, fruit from the Frigidaire, a candlestick there. I watch as she carefully arranges everything on the corner of my dining room table, then stands back and squints at her handiwork.

She holds her hands at arm's length, makes a box with her fingers, and squints through that. Not satisfied, she walks into the kitchen, looks around, takes an empty wine bottle from the trash, and places it on its side in the foreground.

One more squint and she declares, "O. K., that's great. We're ready."

"What do you mean, we're ready?" I ask. "You have too much junk there. I'm not going to paint all that."

Ilene smiles. She's won. I have just made a commitment to paint.

She goes out to her car and drags in her art paraphernalia. I don't help.

She places a sheet of canvas paper on the table in front of me. "First sketch in the shapes," she instructs. "Do it quickly. Don't worry about neatness."

Don't worry about neatness? That I like. I launch into my new career with a bit more enthusiasm.

Two hours of constant work pass.

"That's it. I've had enough," I declare.

"No, no, just the wine bottle in front and you'll be finished," my slave driver insists.

I grouse.

Ilene leaves the room and goes into the bathroom.

As soon as she's gone, I remove the wine bottle from the display. There, now I'm done, I tell myself.

The painting, such as it is, does look unfinished though. A scissors on the buffet catches my eye. I cut an outline of the wine bottle out of the bottom of the canvas paper, then I use some books to prop the painting up on the table top and position the real bottle on its side in front of the outline. I stand back. It took two seconds to do and, to my untrained eye, it's pretty good.

Ilene returns. She stares.

"Ethyl, I can't believe it. That's perfect. Such creativity." She's really excited.

"Come off it, Ilene," I scoff. "You know darn well I did it because I was too lazy to paint in the bottle."

Ilene looks at me haughtily. "It does not make any difference why you do something. It is what you do that makes you an artist."

Here we go again—another lecture about my latent artistic ability.

1977

1-7-1-6, I dial. I know I should wait until after eight o'clock when the lower long distance rates go into effect, but that's hours away. This is too good to keep. I continue dialing the number.

"I couldn't wait to tell you," I greet my sister when she answers the telephone.

"Will we see it here?" she explodes.

We both laugh. We've gone through this routine before. Ilene knows that there is only one reason I call her before the reduced evening rates. To celebrate my getting a commercial. She always skips the preliminaries and gets right to the point, "Will it run on Buffalo television?"

My commercial acting career was as unexpected as it is pleasurable. Two years ago, a friend who owns a cosmetic firm was invited to discuss the proper application of makeup on several television talk shows.

"I need a face to demonstrate on," she told me. "Do you want to come on the shows with me?" I was delighted.

"Do you realize how lucky you are?" an actress friend asked. "You'll be eligible to join Screen Actors Guild. Membership in that is hard to come by."

I called Ilene.

Her first question was, "Will we see it in Buffalo?"

"No, I'm afraid not. It's local," I told her, "but I just found out that I can join the actor's union if I want to."

That's all Ilene had to hear. "It's a sign from above," she proclaimed and immediately started planning a course of action for my new career.

"Wait a minute, Ilene," I interrupted, "so far my crowning acting achievement was that lead in *Cry Havoc* at Ohio State a hundred years ago. I don't think I qualify."

Although she would have liked to proceed full steam ahead, Ilene grudgingly agreed. Then regaining momentum she declared, "But that's easily overcome. Quick, sign up for acting classes. Trust me. I know an omen when I hear one. This is meant to be." The more she talked, the more enthusiastic I became.

Convinced that Hollywood was not looking for another middle-aged star, I narrowed my prospects to television commercials. Ilene was as excited as I when I won my first part.

She is my most avid fan, which is true loyalty considering she's never seen me on TV. The closest I've ever come to showing in Buffalo was several months ago when I was in a commercial that ran in Minneapolis.

Ilene once read in a magazine article about Sandy Duncan's meteoric rise from a bank commercial to Hollywood stardom. She's convinced that I, too, am on the threshold of making it big. She has never stopped expecting that one day she would look at her television set and see me looking back at her. I've always hoped she would, too, but it won't be this time.

"It's going to show in the Cleveland area," I inform her.

"At least you're getting closer. Yesterday Minnesota, today Ohio, tomorrow the world," she laughs. "You wait and see. It will happen."

"Sure," I tell my sister, the eternal optimist.

Assemblage IV

"Where do you live now? I wish you were here."
The Secret Garden

Prologue

1979

The nurses' station is a pool of light in the dark, hushed, hospital corridor. I stand at the high counter just outside the lighted circle, waiting. The night nurse sits at her desk center-stage. Her uniform gleams iridescent in the bright spotlight. She pores over a sheaf of papers, Ilene's hospital records. I stare at the top of her bowed head.

Minutes pass. The nurse stirs. I spring to attention. She glances at the watch on her wrist. As if to verify her findings she turns and looks up at the clock high on the wall beside her. Her face is now bathed in light. Her upturned eyes sparkle. Her hair glows and becomes a halo around her face. She looks like a painting of the Madonna at prayer.

Finally, she turns to me with a faint smile. "I understand that Mrs. Katz is in pain," she says kindly, "but she isn't due for another shot for an hour. I can't give it to her sooner. Morphine is addictive, you know."

The tableau shatters. The spell is broken.

"What difference does it make?" I rasp. I don't recognize my own voice.

1937

I open my eyes. The sun is streaming in the window. I look over at Ilene's twin bed, but she is already gone. She must be downstairs eating breakfast. I hurry to get dressed so I can go down and tell her. She will be so happy. I can't believe I didn't think of it sooner.

It all started two weeks ago. That's when Ilene read that article in the Ladies' Home Journal. She had always been as interested in the Bobbsey twins as I am. The day she read that magazine, though, everything changed. I guess the article really hit home. It was all about the "middle child syndrome." Ever since she read it, Ilene has used it to the hilt. Any time our parents reprimand her she recites verbatim the information she gleaned. "I'm the middle child," she recites, "Dina gets the new clothes, I get the hand-me-downs. She always makes me get out of the living room when her friends come over and you don't even say anything to her. You treat Jerry as if he's a prince. He can do no wrong. You always blame me when I hit him back 'cause he hit me. Do you know what you're doing to my psyche?"

"It is so awful being the middle child," Ilene confides in me periodically. I sympathize and try to find the right words to help mend her wounded psyche.

Finally I am dressed. I hurry downstairs to the kitchen. Ilene is finishing her shredded wheat.

"Ilene," I begin excitedly, "I don't know why I didn't think of it sooner. I just figured something out. I'm a middle child, too."

She stops chewing. "What are you talking about?" She seems annoyed.

I explain, "If Dina is the oldest and Jerry the youngest, that makes me a middle child, too. We're both middle children."

"You are not!" she shouts. "I'm the middle child. Don't you try to horn in."

I'm amazed. I try reasoning with her. She won't listen. She won't even look at me. What's the matter with her? She's not making any sense.

She eats another spoonful of cereal and drops her spoon into the empty bowl. Then she gets up and stalks out of the room without another word.

1987

I walk briskly down the sidewalk toward the restaurant where friends and I have planned to meet for lunch. The Santa Monica autumn leaves scrunching under my feet don't seem to be as crisp as those in Niagara Falls, but I'll take what I can get. Two women walk toward me. They are deep in conversation. As they near they throw their heads back in animated laughter. They are not even aware of me as we pass. I glance back at them over my shoulder with envy. That was us, I think.

Ilene and I near the restaurant where the shower is to take place. We hardly notice the sun dappled sidewalk, we are so intent on our good-natured squabble. We are arguing about which of us had the more difficult childhood.

"I'm telling you, you had it easier," I insist. "It was no fun always hearing Mom's friends arguing about who was prettier, Dina or you. No one even mentioned my name."

"I had it worse," Ilene insists. "All you had to do was wait until you aged. It may have taken you longer than most, but even you outgrew your gawkiness. I spent my entire youth trying to develop a personality like my damn kid sister. You tell me you envied me?"

I wish I'd known then that she thought I had a great personality. It may have made being the only non-beauty in the family easier. "Ugly ducklings develop personality to compensate for what they lack in looks," I joke. "It's something that can't be learned. You either have it or you don't."

"You wait till now to tell me? Where were you when I needed you?" she asks.

"Nurturing my damaged ego. Where were you?"

"Developing a complex of my own."

On the busy sidewalk that sunny afternoon, passersby stepped aside to let two laughing women enter the cool shade of the restaurant. They may have given a fleeting thought to why the two were so jovial.

They will never know. I will never forget.

1941

I am throwing caution to the wind—daring to live dangerously. Soon I will graduate from Niagara Falls High School. Then it will be too late. So, today, I am playing hooky with five of my best high school friends. It's now or never.

The six of us chip in for gas and hightail it the thirty-five miles to Buffalo in Chet Cleveland's car. We have a ball shopping for favors for an upcoming dance, eating donuts for lunch, and cruising around Buffalo. We could have done it on a Saturday, but a school day is much more exciting.

It is now four o'clock. The adventure is over. I have been dropped off at home and am the picture of innocence as I walk in the door with my schoolbooks under my arm.

One look at my Mother and my heart sinks. I can drop my act. It won't save me now.

"Your Father got a call from your principal today," she announces. "I'll tell you now, he is very upset." Mom stares at me for a moment. "Why didn't you learn from what happened to Ilene?" she admonishes.

She sounds almost sympathetic. Obviously, she remembers that day four years ago as well as I do.

I remember opening the door. I could tell immediately that something horrible was happening upstairs. I heard a jumble of voices, all of them yelling. Loudest was my Dad's. "There will be no sneaks in this family. You are disgracing the Nimelman name," he shouted above the din.

I sprinted up the stairs and saw a terrible sight. In the doorway of my bedroom was Dad trying to burst through a wall of human bodies. Dina and Mom were both in the doorway trying desperately to bar his entry into the room. My kid brother Jerry was lying flat on the floor in the hall with his arms wrapped tightly around one of Dad's legs. My God, I remember thinking, if Dad takes one step backward, Jerry is mincemeat.

Through the maze of arms and heads I tried to see what was causing the commotion. On her twin bed in the room we shared was my fifteen year old sister Ilene. She was cowering against the wall, eyes like saucers, too frightened to cry. Without thinking, I sprawled on the floor beside my brother and grabbed Dad's other leg.

"She skipped school today," Jerry yelled. "They called Dad."

Dad, by now, had realized that the only way to reach Ilene was over the dead bodies of his entire family. In frustration, he turned, breaking our chokeholds on his legs. He ran the few steps into the bathroom and grabbed the first thing he saw, a bar of soap. In no time he was back at the guarded bedroom door. As if in slow motion I saw the bar of soap sail across the room. It hit the wall above Ilene's head, ricocheted to the side wall, flew across the room, hit the opposite wall, and finally slid along the floor between our twin beds. Even Dad seemed shocked at what he had done.

His anger spent and, we all hoped, realizing what his fury might have done had his aim been better, Dad turned and stalked down the stairs muttering, "No child of mine is going to be a sneak."

Now, I think, here I am in danger of the same fate, but with no siblings around to guard me. I, too, have broken the Nimelman code of ethics. A Nimelman does not lie, cheat, smoke, steal, swear, nor—obviously—sneak.

Suddenly, I hear Dad's car door slam.

I dart up the stairs. I hear Dad in hot pursuit. I make a mad dash into the bathroom and lock the door. No way is that bar of soap going to be where he can reach it.

Dad is pounding on the bathroom door and I hear his familiar shout. "A Nimelman doesn't sneak. I am not raising hoodlums."

Somehow it doesn't sound as formidable as it did four years ago. Is it the locked door between us? Is it the inaccessible bar of soap? Has Dad mellowed over the years or have I changed?

Dad has stopped pounding and I hear him walking slowly away. His footsteps on the stairs seem more plodding than I remember them. I guess he really has mellowed.

I know I should feel lucky. I got off a lot easier than Ilene. Then why am I sad? I feel a sudden urge to shout through the locked door, "I'm sorry, Dad." But I don't.

1988

    I punch 1-7-1-6 on the telephone keys. Turning my back on the early afternoon sunlight streaming through the window, I continue punching and smile, remembering how it used to be.

    A click on the phone and Terri's, "Hello" jars me and jerks me back to reality. I pause for a moment to regain my equilibrium. I can hear Terri's kids playing in the background.

    "Hi, Terr," I finally greet.

    Terri hears my voice. "Will we see it here in Buffalo?" she asks without preamble.

    Like mother like daughter, I think silently.

    "Yes, you will," I hear myself rasp.

    Damn, I'd meant to keep it light. I try again.

    "It's for Minolta camera. It's going to play all over the country…even Buffalo," I joke weakly.

    There is silence.

    Across the miles we embrace.

1967

We are at the Hollywood Beach Hotel in Florida for the John Hancock Insurance Company convention. Al has been their general agent in Buffalo for many years. Sam and I moved to California two years ago so that Sam could open an office in Beverly Hills for their western division. Ilene and I now live a continent apart.

Sam and Al feel guilty about separating us so they don't complain about the routine Ilene and I have established in order to cope. We each visit the other at least once a year, with or without husbands—their choice. We talk on the telephone whenever one of us feels the need, which is often. We have a reunion at a luxury hotel each year—compliments of John Hancock.

"Let's face it. We see these people just once a year," I tell Ilene while we wait in the lobby for our husbands to check the posted schedule of events. "After 'hello, how are you,' and 'you're looking great,' there's not a lot to talk about. In fact," I continue, "every year on the way to convention, I have to look over the list of attendees to relearn the wives' names. At least I used to until I figured out that if I called everyone Barbara, or slurred over Joan/Jean/Jane, I had covered three quarters of the women here."

Ilene laughs.

She loves going to the conventions. I think the conventions are O.K., mainly because they give me an opportunity to spend time with my sister. Even though there's a huge crowd, we always manage to spend some time alone together. Our convention reunion would work out even better if it weren't for a quirk in Ilene's personality. She loves to socialize with the immediate world.

For the fifteen years she and Al have been attending, Ilene has thrown herself into each convention with gusto. She has gone with Al to every morning business session. For fifteen years! Eight years ago Sam joined the company and we started attending conventions. For several years, I automatically followed Ilene's example and dutifully appeared at each morning session. Then it occurred to me to wonder why. Since then I go to hear the keynote speaker but otherwise I meet the three of them in time for lunch.

"You're so lazy," Ilene accuses.

"You're so gung-ho," I answer.

Ilene doesn't let up in the afternoon, either. While the fellows are at workshops and seminars, I sit by the pool and loaf. In fact, I keep my eyes closed half the time so I don't have to converse with anyone. In the meantime, Ilene flits around poolside fraternizing with all the other spouses.

"It's not coincidental," I tell her, "that you're in bed with a migraine for two days after every convention."

She doesn't listen. She really enjoys being head cheerleader.

Evenings are the same. Each of the four nights of the convention there is a banquet or party. Ilene is the self-appointed hostess and honored guest all rolled into one. Sometimes it's downright embarrassing. From across the length of the ballroom, I can often hear Ilene greeting fellow conventioneers as if each is her long-lost favorite relative. Sam hears her, too. He rolls his eyes. "Why does she have to be so…so…out there?" he asks. I give him a withering look and don't reply. It's all right if I criticize my sister, but I won't allow anyone else to do it. I wait until Sam can't see me and sidle up to her. "Cool it," I whisper. "Let the home office people make sure everyone is having a good time. It's their job, not yours. You're so gung-ho."

"You're so lazy," she whispers back.

We sometimes squabble about our different approaches to life. I tell Ilene that her bubbling enthusiasm is often so over the top that it comes off as phony and that it's also injurious to her health. Ilene tells me that my laid back attitude is an excuse for being lazy and is also antisocial.

Even as we make these accusations, we know. Ilene knows that when she is confronted with a problem that requires logic rather than zeal to solve, she can turn to her down-to-earth sister for a rational perspective and help in finding a solution. I know that there is no one who can anticipate as accurately as she when I need a pat on the back, a slap on the wrist, or a push from behind.

We hear a call from across the lobby, "Hi, Ilene. Hi, Ethyl."

Ilene springs into action. "Hi, Jean! It's good to see you. When did you get in? You're looking great."

1936—Part One

I hear Mom's footsteps on the stairs. She comes through the dining room where I am sitting and heads toward the kitchen. I turn my head the other way. "Your program 'Mert and Marg' is on," she tells the back of my head. "Ilene is in there listening to it." Then she disappears through the doorway into the kitchen to get dinner ready. A minute later I hear her humming and banging pots and pans around.

For fifteen minutes I've been sitting here all alone and miserable and no one has even noticed. A lot anyone around here cares about me. Tears run down my cheeks and off my chin. I wipe them off the polished mahogany table top with my sleeve.

After school today Mom had asked, "Ethyl, do you feel O.K.? Why are you so quiet?"

I was ashamed to tell her my problem right out. "I'm not sick or anything like that," I answered, but I moped while I said it. She didn't even notice. She picked up the phone and called Mrs. Passer. I would have told her, too, if she had only coaxed me a little bit.

For two weeks now, I've kinda guessed but wasn't positive. Now I know. Ilene has a new best friend. Her name is Marion Connelly. If Ilene's not talking to Marion on the telephone, she's talking about her. Ilene and Marion are both in ninth grade. I'm in seventh. Lately, whenever I pass Ilene in the hall, she and Marion are walking with their arms linked and they are gabbing away. They still let me sit with them in the cafeteria but they hardly ever talk to me. They wouldn't even notice if I didn't show up.

Before Marion, I always used to give Ilene half of my mashed potatoes at lunch because she likes them so much. She would always give me licks of her ice cream sucker after I finished mine. But no more. The worst part is, Ilene doesn't even notice. She acts as if nothing is wrong.

This morning after breakfast is when I knew for sure. That's when Ilene gave Mom a list of the kids she's inviting to her boy-girl birthday party next Saturday. I waited until Mom and Ilene left the kitchen. Then I picked up the list from the counter and read it. My name wasn't even there. I'm sure. I checked it twice. In the old days, before Marion, Ilene and I would always sit right next to each other at our birthday parties. She would never have a party without me.

It's getting dark in the dining room now. I lay my head on the table. The cool, smooth wood feels good and for some strange reason, strong and comforting. I close my eyes. Suddenly, I'm jarred by a loud voice coming from the living room. It's Ilene. "Everybody there will be fourteen. She's only a kid. She can't come."

Then I hear Mom's voice. "That's final, Ilene, you will either let your sister come or there will be no party."

I can't believe it. All this time Mom knew. She knew and she's on my side. Muffled voices are coming from the living room. I sit silently in the now dark dining room and strain my ears. Suddenly, Ilene bursts into the hall that divides the two rooms. I can hear her tearful sniffling. She stomps up the stairs to our bedroom. I feel sorry that Ilene is sad but when she's wrong, she's wrong. I can hardly wait until I get to the party and she sees how grown up I can be. She'll change her mind then about Marion being such a big deal.

1937

"It's just foolishness, Ilene," I hear Mom reproach. "Last year a bra and nylons, now a girdle. Why in heavens name do you want a girdle? You're just skin and bones."

I stop bouncing my ball against the side of the house so I can listen. Mom and Ilene are in the living room. I'm playing "leany, clapsy" just outside the open window.

I hear Ilene's tearful voice, "I told you, Mom, my stockings are always sagging around my ankles. And just look at the grooves these garters are making in my leg! See? They shut off my circulation."

Good point I cheer silently. Ilene seems to be making headway with Mom, too. Mom is muttering. I can't hear what she's saying, but to me it sounds like she's weakening.

Ilene's voice again. "This leg is numb all the time. There's no blood in it. I can hardly walk on it."

Stop already, I want to holler. Quit while you're ahead. That Ilene, she'll never learn. I've told her and told her but she never knows when to stop nagging. Disgusted, I continue my interrupted game.

"Twirly around," I shout and slam the ball against the side of the house, twirl my hands around each other, and expertly catch the ball as it rebounds.

"Tabaxy." The ball hits the house with a thud. I touch my shoulders with my fingertips and catch it again.

I am very good at sports. Ilene used to be good, too. Now I can beat her almost every time. I beat her in "leeny, clapsy," I beat her in jacks, I beat her in pickup sticks. Ilene has her mind on so many other things these days. She just can't seem to concentrate on games like I can.

It all started last year with the bra episode. Ilene was fourteen then. I still remember. Ilene told Mom that she really needed to wear a bra instead of an undershirt like we've been wearing all our lives. "Everyone in the locker room laughs at me because I'm the only one who still wears one," she whined.

Mom laughed right out loud. Later we heard her whispering to Mrs. Passer about it on the phone. It made Ilene feel bad. I could tell. She had a funny look on her face and wouldn't talk to me when she came into our room. Ilene did O.K. though. In no time at all she got her first bra. She was thrilled even though she had to wear "gay deceivers" to take up all the extra space.

I didn't know it was going to, but it helped me, too. The following July when I'd just turned thirteen, Ilene let me wear one of her old bras. Mom saw it on me and without blinking an eye said to me, "That bra is a mess. Don't wear underwear like that. What if you were in an accident and went to the hospital? Get rid of that horrible thing. Go buy a new one." I didn't even have to ask.

I continue my game. "Touch your heel," I singsong. Bang goes the ball.

"Touch your toe."

"Touch the ground."

"And under you go," I finish triumphantly. I raise one leg and toss the ball under it then catch it just in time.

Through the corner of my eye I see Ilene coming out the side door. Her face is tear stained but she's grinning ear to ear. She's won! Good going, Ilene. This means that in eight months I'll be wearing a girdle, too, and I won't even be fifteen yet.

1936—Part Two

It's Ilene's fourteenth birthday. I feel a little funny about being here.

I'm sitting all by myself on a corner of the sofa untangling the fringe on one of the arm covers Mom crocheted for our living room furniture. All the other girls are standing in a circle, giggling. A little while ago I heard Ilene whisper, "It's not my fault. My Mom made me let her come." I just sat here combing the fringe with my fingers and pretending I didn't hear her.

The boys are bunched up on the other side of the living room whooping and hollering. They are holding a dirty shoe up in the air and are passing it from one to the other. A real short guy who is all sweated up keeps yelling and hopping up and down trying to get it back. Boy, is Ilene lucky Mom's in the kitchen and can't see this. Mom would throw a fit. I feel sorry for the short kid but I can't help him. No one would listen to me. I wish Ilene would stop giggling long enough to do something about it.

Finally Ilene starts organizing a game. A game of post office. That's not exactly what I had in mind but it's better than sitting here watching the girls act like jerks and the boys pick on the little guy. Ilene has everybody sit in a big circle and gives each one a secret number.

83

Ned, a boy who has a mad crush on Ilene, goes first. He calls my number. My heart does flip-flops. I've never kissed a strange boy before. I don't even know how.

Ned follows me into the dark sun parlor. The only light is that coming through the wall of windows from the street lamp in front of the house. It filters through the leaves of Mom's rubber plants and casts their shadows on the opposite wall and over the cabbage roses on the wicker sofa. I've never seen our sun parlor look so beautiful.

Ned treats me very nice. He doesn't even seem annoyed that he got stuck with me. He gives me a peck on the cheek, then he whispers, "What's Ilene's number?"

"Ten," I whisper back.

"Don't tell anyone else," he begs.

"You can trust me, I won't," I assure him.

He smiles.

I feel important.

Bob, who is sitting beside Ned in the circle, is the next boy to call a number. He picks mine, too. After a quick peck on the cheek, he asks me for Marion's number.

Word spreads. I become the Mata Hari of post office. Each boy gives me the obligatory peck before seeking secret information.

Some of the girls look miffed. "Why do they all want to kiss her? She's only twelve," I hear one of them whisper to Ilene. I just smile. I like being popular.

The next morning when I come downstairs Mom is dusting the living room. "Did you have a good time at Ilene's party?" she asks.

"It was super," I answer. "The girls weren't so nice, but I was popular with all the boys. I liked them a lot."

Mom's dust cloth stops in midair.

Assemblage V

"There is magic in there—good magic—I am sure there is."

The Secret Garden

Prologue

Ilene's hand rests lightly in mine on the white sheet. She gazes through the window across from her hospital bed at the treetops covered with early spring buds. No blankets cover her. She looks beautiful in her flowing silk nightgown. A narrow band of ecru lace lines the neck, long sleeves, and hem. Her feet are bare.

I ask if she is chilly. She turns to look at me, smiles, then turns back to watch the swaying branches. Moments later, still staring out the window, she says quietly, "We'll meet in our secret garden."

"I know," I reply.

I open my eyes. Darkness surrounds me and I hear Sam's rhythmic breathing beside me.

Flowing nightgown? Lace trim? Blossoming trees? If only it had been that way. If only life was that kind. I am fully awake now. "It was a dream, only a dream," I whisper.

I lie staring into space reviewing every detail of it so I will remember in the morning.

1931

"Come on, Ilene, please tell me," I beg.

"I would if I could but I can't," she sing-songs. "It's a secret society. You don't belong, so I can't tell you." She turns and walks away.

"I'm going to be a member soon," I plead, following her. "It isn't my fault that you grabbed the label from the Ovaltine can first." In fact, Ilene helped me talk Mom into getting another one before hers was empty. "I'll be getting my decoder pin any day now. Then I'll be a member, too," I whine to her back.

Ilene ignores me.

I take my final shot. "If Little Orphan Annie knew, I bet she'd say it's O.K."

Ilene stops and thinks about that. "I'll tell you what I'll do," she finally says. "I won't tell you what it is, but when I decode my message, I'll give you a hint and you can try to figure it out. That way I won't really be breaking my Little Orphan Annie Secret Society pledge."

My sister is so good to me, I think. Leave it to her to find a way to help me without breaking her oath.

"O.K.," I agree eagerly.

That decided, we lie down on the living room rug in front of Mom's big Spartan radio. It has beautiful dragons carved on the outside of the cabinet doors. We can't see them now because the doors are open.

We sing along with the announcer:
> "Always wears a sunny smile,
> Now wouldn't it be worth your while,
> If you could be,
> Like Little Orphan Annie."

For the next fifteen minutes we listen intently.

The program is soon over and we hear the announcer say, "All right, all you members of Orphan Annie's Secret Society, get ready for your secret message. Do you have a pencil and paper ready? Here are the numbers for today."

Ilene writes them all down on her tablet. Then she goes and sits on the couch. I sit on the floor and watch her as she goes back and forth, turning the wheel on her decoder pin and then writing something in her tablet. When she finishes, she puts her pencil on the coffee table and, holding the tablet close to her chest, silently reads what she has written.

"Is it good or bad?" I ask eagerly.

She frowns.

Does that mean it's bad or that I shouldn't have asked, I wonder.

"Is it about Annie?"

She frowns.

"Daddy Warbucks?"

She frowns.

"Sandy?"

She smiles, sadly.

I got it. It's about Sandy, and it's bad.

"Sandy gets killed?"

She looks disgusted.

"He dies?"

She still looks disgusted.

"He gets lost?"

There's that sad smile again.

"My God! How terrible! Do they find him?" I beg.

Ilene finally breaks her silence. "How do I know? They don't tell me everything!"

1934—Part One

Just like last year. Mom, Ilene, and me. We are seated on the same wooden folding chairs Mrs. Quinan always borrows from Gridley's Funeral Home for the annual piano recital. She lines them up in neat rows in her living room. It's a little spooky when you first walk in and see GRIDLEY'S MORTUARY stamped in bold black letters on the back of each chair. But when all of Mrs. Quinan's other victims and their mothers are seated the letters don't show.

Mrs. Quinan is making her usual welcoming speech. She drones on and on. Here we go again, I think wearily, and drift slowly into my own private world.

Suddenly, I am jarred from my reverie by the bold opening chords of Rachmaninoff's Prelude in D Flat Minor. Good, I have missed most of Mrs. Quinan's speech. Her prize student, Jean Ruth, has taken center stage. Jean plays with her head cocked as if she's hearing each chord for the very first time. Her eyes are half closed and each time she strikes a chord her head swings violently up and down and her hair flies all over her face. She sure is pounding up a storm.

It reminds me of the good old days before Mrs. Quinan. Ilene and I would take turns pounding on Mom's baby grand piano while the other stood and watched the hammers hit the wires inside. Sometimes we'd sit side by side on the piano bench and play chopsticks.

We've been taking lessons for two years. We hate the lessons but love the two duets Mrs. Quinan picked for us to play in the recital this year. One is slow and dreamy. The other is like a Sousa march. There is one part in the march that I like a lot, even though I had to practice it over and over to get it right. For several bars Ilene stops playing, I do a brisk solo, strike a chord, Ilene joins in again, and we finish with a flourish.

I am jarred from my private thoughts this time by Mrs. Quinan, who is announcing my name. I had better pay attention. I follow Ilene to the front of the room. We play our dreamy duet without a glitch. Not as dramatically as Jean Ruth, of course, but we do well. We take our uncomfortable seats again beside Mom. She is smiling proudly. At least she seems happy, I think. How could she have forgotten so soon our bitter clash just last night? Ilene and I had ganged up on her.

"I don't want to be in Mrs. Quinan's old recital," I had whined.

"I hate Mrs. Quinan, I hate practicing, I hate the piano," Ilene picked up where I left off. "I want to take guitar or maybe tap dancing like everyone else. You kept telling us that some day we'd thank you. Well, it's been two years and neither of us has ever thanked you."

Mom completely ignored our tirades and stated quietly, "You will both be in that recital tomorrow night."

Mom was right. Here we are.

I become aware of Mrs. Quinan's voice again. "Now we will hear from the Nimelman sisters again, playing their final number."

Ilene and I seat ourselves on the piano bench and begin to play. We're good. I imagine everyone in the audience wanting to clap hands in time with our syncopated march. Then it happens. At the very end of my short solo, just as I am about to strike my big chord, I find that my fingers are in all the wrong positions. I can't go on. I panic. But I can't just sit here. I start hitting any old keys. It reminds me of the times Ilene and I pounded on the piano to watch the hammers hit the wires. And it sounds like it too. Ilene is dumbfounded. Finally though, she reads my mind. We both pick up where she joins in again, and finish with our usual flourish.

One week later. Tuesday, 3 p.m. Time for our piano lesson. Ilene and I say nothing. Mom says nothing. Mrs. Quinan doesn't even call. Perhaps she realizes how prophetic her introduction was when she announced at the recital that the Nimelman sisters would play their final duet.

A few days after that Mom lowered the piano top so the hammers and the wires don't show anymore. She now has a big, black satin Spanish shawl draped over the whole top. It has bright flowers embroidered all over it and has fringe hanging from its edges. On it she has placed pictures of everyone in the family in pretty silver frames.

Sometimes I hear Mom lament to Dad, "That big, beautiful piano and all it's used for is to decorate the living room!" Ilene and I think it looks great.

1933

Here we are sitting straight up in the back seat. We don't dare lean back, we're wearing our brand new matching dresses. Well, almost matching. Ilene's is white organdy with brown polka dots and mine is white organdy with red polka dots. Mom likes to dress us this way even though we're not twins. We have on our white gloves, too. Dad is driving us to City Hall. We're going on very important business. Dad said that he had something to do downtown anyway, so he would take us if we were sure we wanted to go.

Dad parks the car at the bottom of the long row of stone steps that lead up to City Hall. The three of us climb the stairs and enter the lobby.

"The man over there will tell you which office it is," Dad says. "I'll wait for you right here."

Why is the man looking at us so funny? All we asked him was which way to go. And why is he looking over at Dad like that? It's the same look Mom had when Dad told her where we were going.

We open the door the man points to and go in.

"We're here to see the Mayor," I announce to the woman behind the desk.

There's that look again. What's the matter with everyone today?

"You don't have an appointment," she says, "let me ask if he can fit you in."

She returns in no time.

"The Mayor will see you."

She seems surprised.

We walk into the longest room I've ever seen. It has a desk way at the other end. Sitting at the desk is—my God, it's him—the man who waves from the big car at the front of all the Memorial Day parades, the picture on the front page of the Niagara Falls Gazette. Why did I tell Dad I wanted to come? What am I doing here?

I scoot behind Ilene and follow her across the long room. I walk so close to her my shoes make black smudges on the backs of her white maryjanes. My eyes glue themselves to the green rug. I see a big pair of black shoes come over to meet us.

A booming voice says, "What can I do for you, ladies?"

I can't make my eyes come unglued from the black shoes on the green rug. My tongue is stuck to the top of my mouth. My lips are so dry they won't open.

At last I hear Ilene's jaunty voice. "We want to open a lemonade stand in Hyde Park. Dad says we can't until we get a City permit from you."

I hear the black shoes chuckle. Good, he likes our idea.

"We had a stand yesterday in front of our house," Ilene continues, "but we only made ten cents and half of it was from Mom. Dad says it's because no one ever passes our house. He says we need a better spot. You know, like Hyde Park."

The black shoes chuckle again. That's a good sign.

But then, "I'd like to help you out but there's already a big stand there. They pay the City a lot of money not to let anyone else open one. I'm really very sorry." He sounds as if he means it.

His black shoes walk us to the door.

Dad is waiting for us in the lobby. He walks between us down the stairs.

"Well, how did it go," he asks.

"He said 'no,'" Ilene chirps as she bounces from step to step, "but he was really sorry. I like him."

"Me, too," I volunteer before he has time to ask. I don't dare take my eyes off the stairs. You could get killed if you fell.

1934—Part Two

"We greet thee Cuba, land of flower, dee-dah-dee-dah," Ilene and I wail as we hula from opposite corners to meet in the middle of the living room. We sidestep all the way to make certain that our backs are never turned to the sofa where our audience will be seated.

We stopped taking piano lessons after our recital fiasco. I guess Mom just gave up on us. Ilene and I don't care. We dance now. We make up wonderful routines, practice them, and then put on shows for Mom and Dad. We're working on one now.

"Why do we have to use a song that I've never heard?" I complain. "You don't even know all the words, and you don't know the tune, either."

"Because we need something tango-ish for our show," Ilene explains. "All of our other dances look alike."

"Is the hula tango-ish?" I ask.

"Close enough," she assures me.

Satisfied, I turn my attention back to inventing our dance. I've got a feel for it now. "I know, I'll take a rose out of my hair and put it between my teeth," I invent as we go along. "You bend me back over your arm till my hair touches the floor. That will look great. Let's try it."

Ilene pauses. "I want to be the one who bends. My hair is longer," she pouts.

"You can't. You're not double-jointed like I am," I retort. "I can bend back much further than you." Ilene knows when she's beaten and concedes.

Last week I found out that I have a special talent. I was doing tricks for Mom. One of them was lying on my stomach and touching my toes to the back of my head. Mom was astounded. "I didn't know that you could do that," she said. "You must be double-jointed." She called Dad into the room. "Look at what Ethyl can do." I did my trick for Dad. "She's double-jointed, all right," he confirmed. I felt proud.

Ilene and I practice our maneuver over and over until we have it perfect. Most of the dance now consists of me weaving my hands in the air in time with the music like we've seen belly dancers do in the movies. All the while, Ilene works at bending me back over her arm and slowly lowering me until my hair sweeps the floor. It looks great but we still have one problem. We've got to find more dancing for Ilene to do. "I've got it," I tell her. "You wear Jerry's cowboy hat. Pretend it's a sombrero. After my bends, you throw the hat on the floor and dance all around it. I'll stamp my feet, swish my skirt, and point at you while you do it."

I wait for Ilene's alternative plan.

"O.K.," she readily agrees. She doesn't even try to alter my idea. She must assume that anyone blessed with double-jointed limbs must also possess superior choreographic ability.

"Now let's take it from the top," I command.

Ilene moves dutifully to her corner of the living room.

I like this. I'm the star *and* director. My creative juices gush. I am heady with power. "For our next routine we'll do that song that goes, 'How you going to keep them down on the farm after they've seen Paree?'" I exclaim. "We'll wear lots of petticoats and can-can. It will be absolutely beautiful."

"Sounds terrific," Ilene declares.

This beats piano any day.

1968

A Sunday in March. Another sunny day in Pacific Palisades, California. Sam and I are sunning on lounges out in back.

"Boy, is Ilene thrilled about the house they're buying," I tell him. "Now I'll forgive Al."

"For what, this time?" Sam asks.

He knows that periodically I get miffed with his brother, usually for some real or imagined slight to my sister.

"You know how excited Ilene was when they found that Frank Lloyd Wright house last month." I tell him, trying to conceal the hostility creeping into my voice. "She wanted that house desperately, but your brother complained, 'It's too sterile. It's too dark.' He was adamant. Ilene and Al really argued about that house. She complained to me about it long distance. I've been mad at Al ever since for being so pig-headed. I couldn't tell Ilene. No use pouring fuel on the fire. But I'll tell you now," I confess, "This whole month, whenever you've mentioned your brother's name, I've made a face behind your back."

Sam laughs. He knows that, although I get annoyed with his brother, it usually doesn't last long.

I can hardly wait to see the house when I visit there next month. They won't be in it yet, but Ilene is going to have the real estate agent make arrangements. All Ilene would tell me about it is that it's near the Albright Knox Art Gallery.

"I remember being in that neighborhood once," I rattle on. "When I was a kid, Ilene took art classes at the Albright. All I remember is that the houses near there are huge."

"Did I ever tell you about the time I went with Ilene to her art class?" I ask.

Sam looks like he's dozing and probably couldn't care less.

"Un-uh," he grunts.

"I was just ten and don't remember much," I begin. "All I do remember is that the day I was there they each did a charcoal drawing of a vase of flowers. I peeked at everyone's and I remember telling Ilene, 'Yours is way better than anyone else's.' An unbiased art connoisseur at ten," I laugh.

Sam chuckles to let me know he's listening.

"What I remember best about that morning was the cookie I had in one of those big houses across the street."

"Huh?" Sam grunts.

"In those days," I explain, "it took almost an hour for Mom to drive Ilene to Buffalo for class. Mom had to get right back to the Falls because Saturday morning was the busiest time of the week in the store. She had to be there by nine and Ilene had to be in class at nine. So Mom had to drop Ilene off early. Do you know what Mom did?"

Sam grunts again.

"She knocked on the door of one of those huge houses across the street and asked if her daughter could sit in their house for an hour on Saturday mornings until the art school opened. A long time later Mom found out that Ilene was spending an hour each week in the home of the Goodyears!"

Sam chuckles.

"Anyway, Mom dropped us off in front of this big house and told us she'd be back as close to noon as she could make it. Ilene knocked on the kitchen door and the maid let us in. Ilene headed straight for a chair by the kitchen table. I was so amazed I just stood there near the door. I didn't even notice that she'd gone. Never had I seen a kitchen like this. Opposite the door was a red brick wall. In the wall, not on the floor, but about as high as my chest, was a fireplace. The fireplace wall was open on both sides. The stove and sink and all that was on the other side. A fireplace in the middle of a kitchen, can you imagine? Not only was there a fireplace in the kitchen, but all the cupboards and some of the walls were made of beautiful dark wood, like the wood on my Mom's living room furniture."

"Finally, I sat in the chair next to Ilene. The maid put two glasses of milk and a plate with two big cookies in front of us. Those cookies smelled so good. 'Watch out, I just took them out of the oven,' the maid warned us. I was shy and felt funny about eating in front of a stranger, so I waited to see what Ilene did. She took a cookie, so I did too. Never in my whole life have I tasted a cookie as good as that one."

"Um," I hear Sam say.

"Then the butler came in and said to Ilene, 'How is our little Rembrandt this morning?' I remember thinking, I like Ilene's new friends, I like the cookies they bake, and I like their house, too.

'Now,' I conclude, 'Ilene and Al are going to live in that neighborhood. Isn't it great?'"

Sam is snoring.

A month later Ilene meets me at the airport. We drive with her real estate agent to the house. It is a tall, stucco house directly across the street from Delaware Park. A man answers when the real estate agent rings. He opens the door wide to let us in.

"No wait," Ilene says dramatically, "May we come in the back door?"

The three of us, Ilene, the agent, and I, troop around to the kitchen door. I imagine the agent thinking, "Wow, is she an eccentric!"

I'm thinking, 'No, it couldn't be.' But I'm suspicious.

Ilene's face is expressionless.

One step inside and my suspicions are confirmed. There is the strange fireplace and the dark wood paneled walls and cupboards like Mom's living room furniture.

"This is it," Ilene laughs. "Do you remember?"

Do I remember! "At long last," I squeal, "I can see the rest of the house."

The man and the real estate agent watch bewildered while two middle-aged women embrace and dance up and down.

1979

"She picked us! Can you believe it?" Ilene whispers excitedly. "With all the wives to choose from, she asked us!"

Ilene and I are at another John Hancock Insurance Company convention, leaving a spouses' luncheon where we sat with a home office V.P. We are hurrying to our adjoining hotel rooms to tell our husbands the news.

"Your wives have been asked to fly all over the country to speak at the spouses' meetings at the three regional Leaders Conventions," Ilene blurts out when we see them. "They want us to discuss the wife's role in the success of her husband's insurance career," she tells our astounded husbands.

"And by the time we finish speaking at John Hancock conventions," I pipe up, "we'll be so good at it we'll get an agent and take our show on the road. We'll travel to speaking engagements all over the country giving inspirational lectures to corporate wives," I finish triumphantly.

"Aren't you getting a little carried away?" Sam asks. He's too late.

In my mind's eye I already see it:

A taxi careens through city traffic toward the airport. Two smartly dressed, beautifully coifed women sit calmly in the back seat. *They are so self-confident that it has not even occurred to them to have a whispered discussion on what the correct tip to the driver should be. They alight at the curb and race to the jet gate just in time to catch a flight to their next speaking engagement.*

Their husbands, back in their respective hometowns, speak with each other long distance about how proud they are of their energetic, emancipated wives.

For the rest of the convention Ilene and I spend every free moment discussing the format of our upcoming debut. Finally we come up with an agenda. We have almost three months. Each of us will write a lecture. In two months Ilene and Al plan to come to California to visit. Ilene will come a few days early. We'll review what each of us has written. More than likely our philosophies will differ. Our emphasis will then be that there is no one "right way" to be a successful helpmate. Then we'll put our heads together to come up with a snappy finish to wind up the talk. We leave the convention confident that we will end up with a worthwhile exchange.

During the next two months I work sporadically on my speech. Several times I call and ask Ilene how she's doing with her writing.

"I haven't been feeling well," she tells me. "But I'll be ready on time, don't worry," she assures me.

A week before Ilene's planned arrival I really start plugging away.

It is now the Tuesday before Ilene is due. I am sitting at the kitchen table putting the finishing touches on my talk. The telephone rings. It is Ilene. Long distance in the middle of the afternoon? This must be important.

"Ethyl, I can't come to California Friday," she begins. "As you know, I haven't been feeling great. Dr. Stine can't find a thing wrong. I have an appointment Thursday with a gastroenterologist. Maybe I'll feel better then."

No preamble. No lilting rush of words tripping over each other to be heard. She speaks matter of factly, flatly. She doesn't sound like Ilene. I glance out the window and wonder why I am shivering. We must be having a sudden chill.

Ilene and I talk seriously for a long time. I press for any facts I may not already know to repeat to doctor friends I will call as soon as we hang up. She talks freely, but quietly.

Finally we say good-bye. I sit, humming phone in hand, staring at my meaningless notes. Suddenly, through the window, I hear a long anguished cry. Startled, I look out. No one is there.

Epilogue

Through my closed eyelids, I see a bright gold light. At last. She has come. I know she's here.

I open my eyes and sure enough—there is the green wicker sofa all filled with huge pink cabbage roses and there are the rubber plants that reach way up to the sky. Best of all, there, sitting in our arm chair smiling at me, is Ilene. She beckons me to come sit in the chair with her. We'll never fit, I think, but I try. To my surprise it's really very comfortable.

I speak urgently but softly. "Ilene, don't you remember? Just before you left me you promised. I remember your exact words. You said, 'We'll meet in our own secret garden.' That's what you said. Knowing you would be here for me whenever I needed you was the only thing that made your going bearable. There have been so many times I've come looking for you, Ilene. Why weren't you ever here?"

I know that I am whining, and I know how much Ilene hates it when I do, but I can't help it. I've got to know.

"That wasn't what I meant," Ilene says. A cloud passes over her face. "The secret garden isn't a place, Ethyl. It isn't rubber plants or cabbage roses on green wicker furniture. It is our 'do you remember when' sessions late at night. It is the conversations we've had at odd moments in unexpected places. It is you knowing that I am there at special family occasions even though we can't speak." She gently

pushes back strands of hair that have tumbled over my eyes. "I'm sorry you misunderstood. I'm sorry it caused you pain."

As quickly as it came, the cloud passes.

"But we are together now, Ethyl." Her smile is tender. "Mom, Dad and the others will be here soon. Let's not waste time bickering. There's so much I can't wait to tell you."

That is what it will be like. I really believe it.